This Is the Way We Go to School

A Book About Children Around the World

This Is the Way We Go to School

A Book About Children Around the World

by EDITH BAER

illustrated by
STEVE BJÖRKMAN

SCHOLASTIC INC.
New York Toronto London Auckland Sydney
Mexico City New Delhi Hong Kong Buenos Aires

To Marta,
and her schoolmates
around the world. — E.B.

ISBN-13: 978-0-590-43162-0
ISBN-10: 0-590-43162-5

Text copyright © 1990 by Edith Baer.

Illustrations copyright © 1990 by Steven Björkman.

58 57 56 55   19/0

Printed in the U.S.A.   40

One by one or two by two —
Come along, it's fun to do!

Ellen takes it nice and slow,

time to watch the flowers grow.

Liz and Larry, as a rule,
wear their jogging shoes to school.

But at twenty minutes past,
roller skates are twice as fast.

And the fastest way by far

is by school bus or by car!

Jenny, Jerry, Pete, and Perry

ride the Staten Island Ferry.

Cable cars take Jack and Jill
up the hill —

and down the hill.

Michael and his friend Miguel
see the rooftops from the El.

Horse-and-buggy rides, it's plain,
start the day for Jake and Jane.

And in Philly, Mitch and Molly
go to school by trackless trolley!

Bianca, Beppo, Benedetto
ride aboard the *vaporetto*.

Bundled up against the breeze,

Niels and Solveig go on skis.

Palm trees help keep Ahmed cool
on his sunny walk to school.

Mira takes time out to play,
school's a hop and skip away.

And watch Sepp and Heidi sail
through the air from peak to vale!

Akinyi leaves for school by train,
far across the mountain chain.

Kay and Fay and Flo and Joe
go to school by radio.

Bicycles bring Mei and Ling
through the traffic of Nanjing.

And beneath the dripping sky,
Ram is riding high and dry.

William comes ashore by boat,
counting sea gulls while afloat.

Carlos takes the town in stride.

Luz prefers the countryside.

And the famous Metro line
suits Igor and Ilyana fine.

Go by Copter?

By Skidoo?
Somewhere, sometimes, some kids do!

You come, too! We'll look for you.

THIS IS WHERE WE LIVE

Ellen lives in Hawaii, U.S.A.

Liz and Larry and the skater live in California, U.S.A.

The bus and car riders live in Raytown, Missouri, U.S.A.

Jenny, Jerry, Pete, and Perry live in Staten Island, New York, U.S.A.

Jack and Jill live in San Francisco, California, U.S.A.

Michael and Miguel live in Chicago, Illinois, U.S.A.

Jake and Jane live in Lancaster, Pennsylvania, U.S.A.

Mitch and Molly live in Philadelphia, Pennsylvania, U.S.A.

Bianca, Beppo, and Benedetto live in Venice, Italy.

Niels and Solveig live in Norway.

Ahmed lives in Egypt.

Mira lives in Israel.

Sepp and Heidi live in Switzerland.

Akinyi lives in Kenya.

Kay, Fay, Flo, and Joe live in Australia.

Mei and Ling live in China.

Ram lives in India.

William lives in Maine, U.S.A.

Carlos and Luz live in Mexico.

Igor and Ilyana live in Moscow, Russia.

The Copter passengers live in Siberia, Russia.

The Skidoo passengers live in Canada.

① Ellen
② Liz and Larry and the skater
③ The bus and car riders
④ Jenny, Jerry, Pete, and Perry
⑤ Jack and Jill
⑥ Michael and Miguel

⑦ Jake and Jane
⑧ Mitch and Molly
⑨ Bianca, Beppo, and Benedetto
⑩ Niels and Solveig
⑪ Ahmed
⑫ Mira

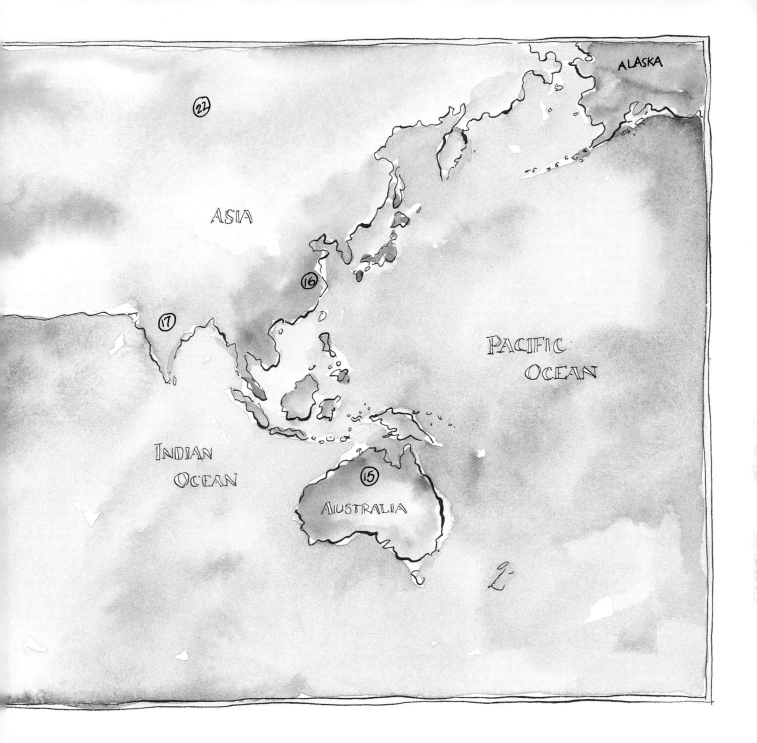

13 Sepp and Heidi
14 Akinyi
15 Kay, Fay, Flo, and Joe
16 Mei and Ling
17 Ram
18 William
19 Carlos
20 Luz
21 Igor and Ilyana
22 The Copter passengers
23 The Skidoo passengers